THE PERIODIC TABLE OF ELEMENTS

ALKALI METALS, ALKALINE EARTH METALS AND TRANSITION METALS

CHILDREN'S CHEMISTRY BOOK

BABY PROFESSOR

EDUCATION KIDS

Speedy Publishing LLC

40 E. Main St. #1156

Newark, DE 19711

www.speedypublishing.com

Copyright 2016

Studying and understanding chemistry gives us the amazing opportunity to get into details of how the world around us works. We come to learn that everything in the universe is made up of matter and elements.

Read on and learn amazing facts about the periodic table of elements and the specific details about alkali metals, alkaline Earth Metals, and transition metals!

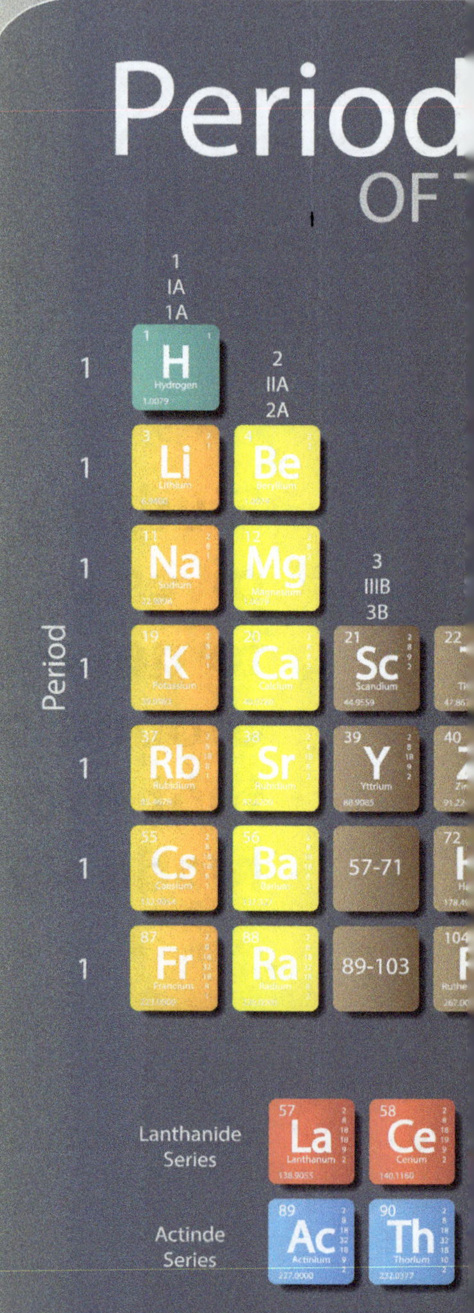

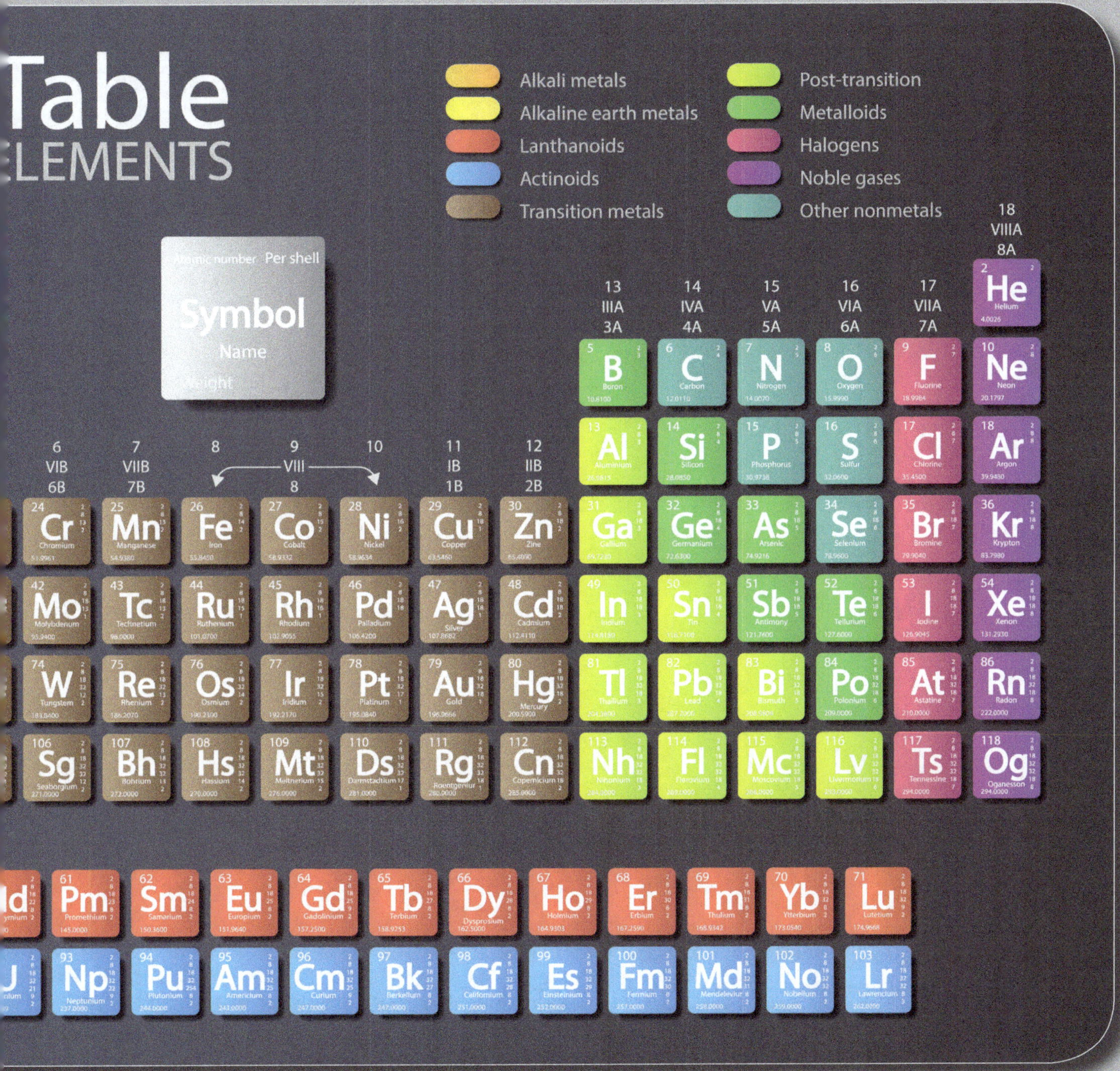

Table
ELEMENTS
Alkali metals
Alkaline earth metals
Lanthanoids
Actinoids
Transition metals
Post-transition
Metalloids
Halogens
Noble gases
Other nonmetals
Atomic number Per shell
Symbol
Name
Weight
18 VIIIA 8A
13 IIIA 3A
14 IVA 4A
15 VA 5A
16 VIA 6A
17 VIIA 7A
2 He Helium 4.0026
5 B Boron 10.8100
6 C Carbon 12.0110
7 N Nitrogen 14.0070
8 O Oxygen 15.9990
9 F Fluorine 18.9984
10 Ne Neon 20.1797
13 Al Aluminium 26.9815
14 Si Silicon 28.0850
15 P Phosphorus 30.9738
16 S Sulfur 32.0600
17 Cl Chlorine 35.4500
18 Ar Argon 39.9480
6 VIB 6B
7 VIIB 7B
8
9 VIII 8
10
11 IB 1B
12 IIB 2B
24 Cr Chromium 51.9961
25 Mn Manganese 54.9380
26 Fe Iron 55.8450
27 Co Cobalt 58.9332
28 Ni Nickel 58.6934
29 Cu Copper 63.5460
30 Zn Zinc 65.4090
31 Ga Gallium 69.7230
32 Ge Germanium 72.6300
33 As Arsenic 74.9216
34 Se Selenium 78.9600
35 Br Bromine 79.9040
36 Kr Krypton 83.7980
42 Mo Molybdenum 95.9400
43 Tc Technetium 98.0000
44 Ru Ruthenium 101.0700
45 Rh Rhodium 102.9055
46 Pd Palladium 106.4200
47 Ag Silver 107.8682
48 Cd Cadmium 112.4110
49 In Indium 114.8180
50 Sn Tin 118.7100
51 Sb Antimony 121.7600
52 Te Tellurium 127.6000
53 I Iodine 126.9045
54 Xe Xenon 131.2930
74 W Tungsten 183.8400
75 Re Rhenium 186.2070
76 Os Osmium 190.2300
77 Ir Iridium 192.2170
78 Pt Platinum 195.0840
79 Au Gold 196.9666
80 Hg Mercury 200.5900
81 Tl Thallium 204.3800
82 Pb Lead 207.2000
83 Bi Bismuth 208.9804
84 Po Polonium 209.0000
85 At Astatine 210.0000
86 Rn Radon 222.0000
106 Sg Seaborgium 271.0000
107 Bh Bohrium 272.0000
108 Hs Hassium 270.0000
109 Mt Meitnerium 276.0000
110 Ds Darmstadtium 281.0000
111 Rg Roentgenium 280.0000
112 Cn Copernicium 285.0000
113 Nh Nihonium 284.0000
114 Fl Flerovium 289.0000
115 Mc Moscovium 288.0000
116 Lv Livermorium 293.0000
117 Ts Tennessine 294.0000
118 Og Oganesson 294.0000
61 Pm Promethium 145.0000
62 Sm Samarium 150.3600
63 Eu Europium 151.9640
64 Gd Gadolinium 157.2500
65 Tb Terbium 158.9253
66 Dy Dysprosium 162.5000
67 Ho Holmium 164.9303
68 Er Erbium 167.2590
69 Tm Thulium 168.9342
70 Yb Ytterbium 173.0540
71 Lu Lutetium 174.9668
93 Np Neptunium 237.0000
94 Pu Plutonium 244.0000
95 Am Americium 243.0000
96 Cm Curium 247.0000
97 Bk Berkelium 247.0000
98 Cf Californium 251.0000
99 Es Einsteinium 252.0000
100 Fm Fermium 257.0000
101 Md Mendelevium 258.0000
102 No Nobelium 259.0000
103 Lr Lawrencium 262.0000

All stuff on Earth is made up of atoms. Basically, atoms are the building blocks of matter and they are made up of protons, neutrons, and electrons.

WHAT IS THE PERIODIC TABLE OF ELEMENTS?

Elements play an amazing role in Chemistry. The elements are listed by the structure of their atoms.

Meitnerium
(266)
110
(269)
111
(272)
61
Pm
62
Sm
Samarium
150.36
63
Eu
Europium
151.964
64
Gd
Gadolinium
157.25
95
Am
Cm
Curium
base
CH3COOH
CO2
O2
hydrolysis
HO
H2N

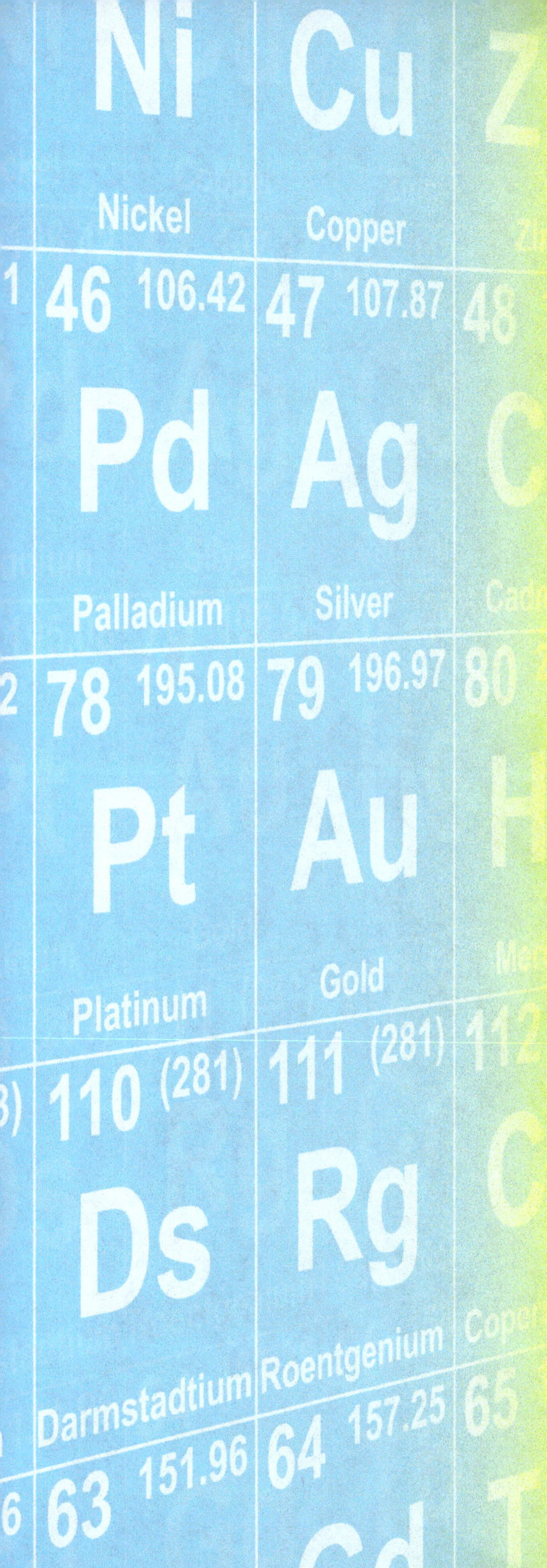

This list is what we call the Periodic Table of Elements. The list of elements includes the number of protons and electrons in their outer shell.

Moreover, the elements in the periodic table are listed according to their atomic number. The atomic number denotes the number of protons in each atom.

7 94
hium
3
Li
6.941
Beryllium
4
Be
9.01
dium
Mo

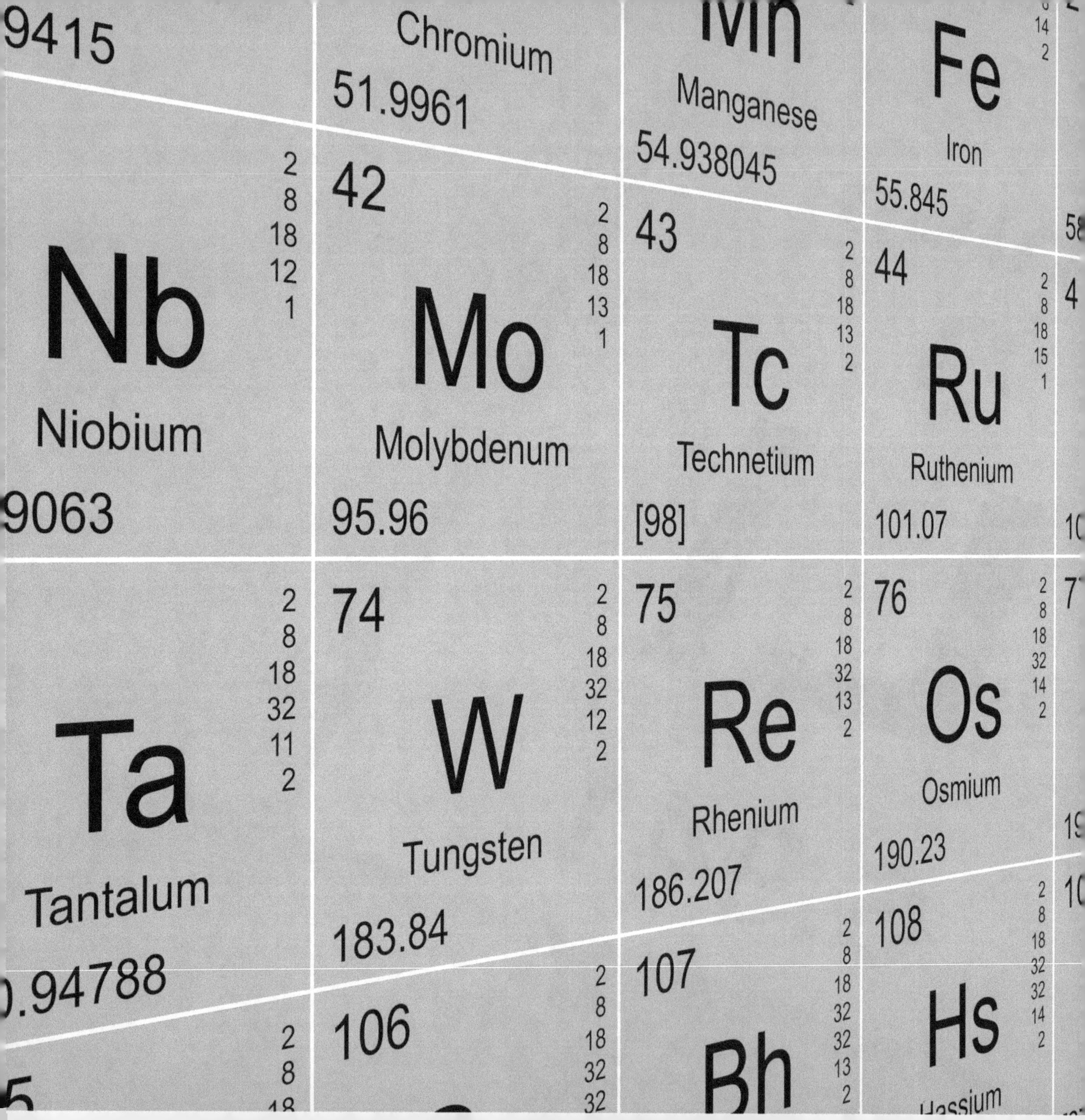
9415
Chromium
51.9961
2
8
18
12
1
42
Nb
Niobium
9063
Mo
Molybdenum
95.96
Mn
Manganese
54.938045
2
8
18
13
1
43
Tc
Technetium
[98]
Fe
Iron
55.845
58
44
2
8
18
13
2
Ru
Ruthenium
101.07
4
10
2
8
18
15
1
74
Ta
Tantalum
.94788
2
8
18
32
11
2
W
Tungsten
183.84
75
2
8
18
32
12
2
Re
Rhenium
186.207
76
2
8
18
32
13
2
Os
Osmium
190.23
7
10
19
2
8
18
32
14
2
106
107
2
8
18
32
32
13
2
Bh
108
2
8
18
32
32
14
2
Hs
Hassium

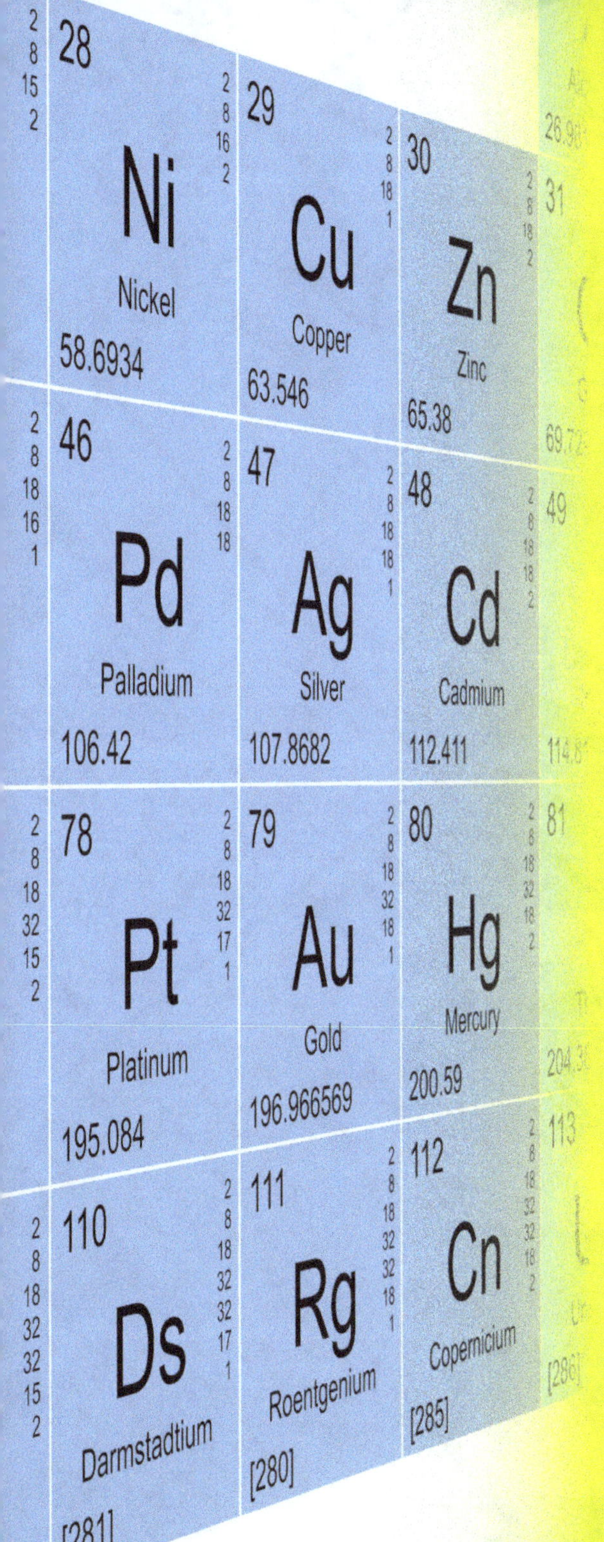

Why is it called Periodic Table of Elements? It is called Periodic Table of Elements because the line-up of elements is in periods or cycles. The period is characterized by the horizontal rows in the table with a total of seven to eight periods.

Elements are lined up in rows, from left to right. The periodic table is the best way to learn elements in Chemistry. This is an impressive guide to learners like you.

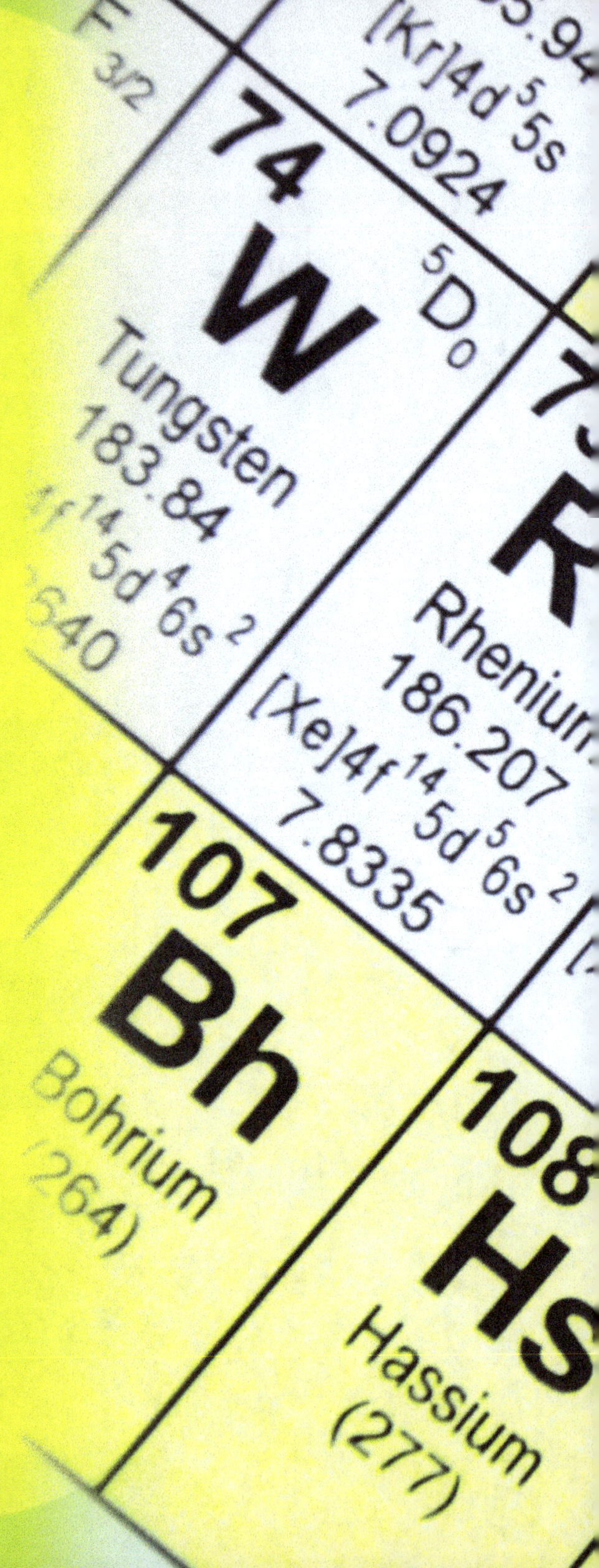

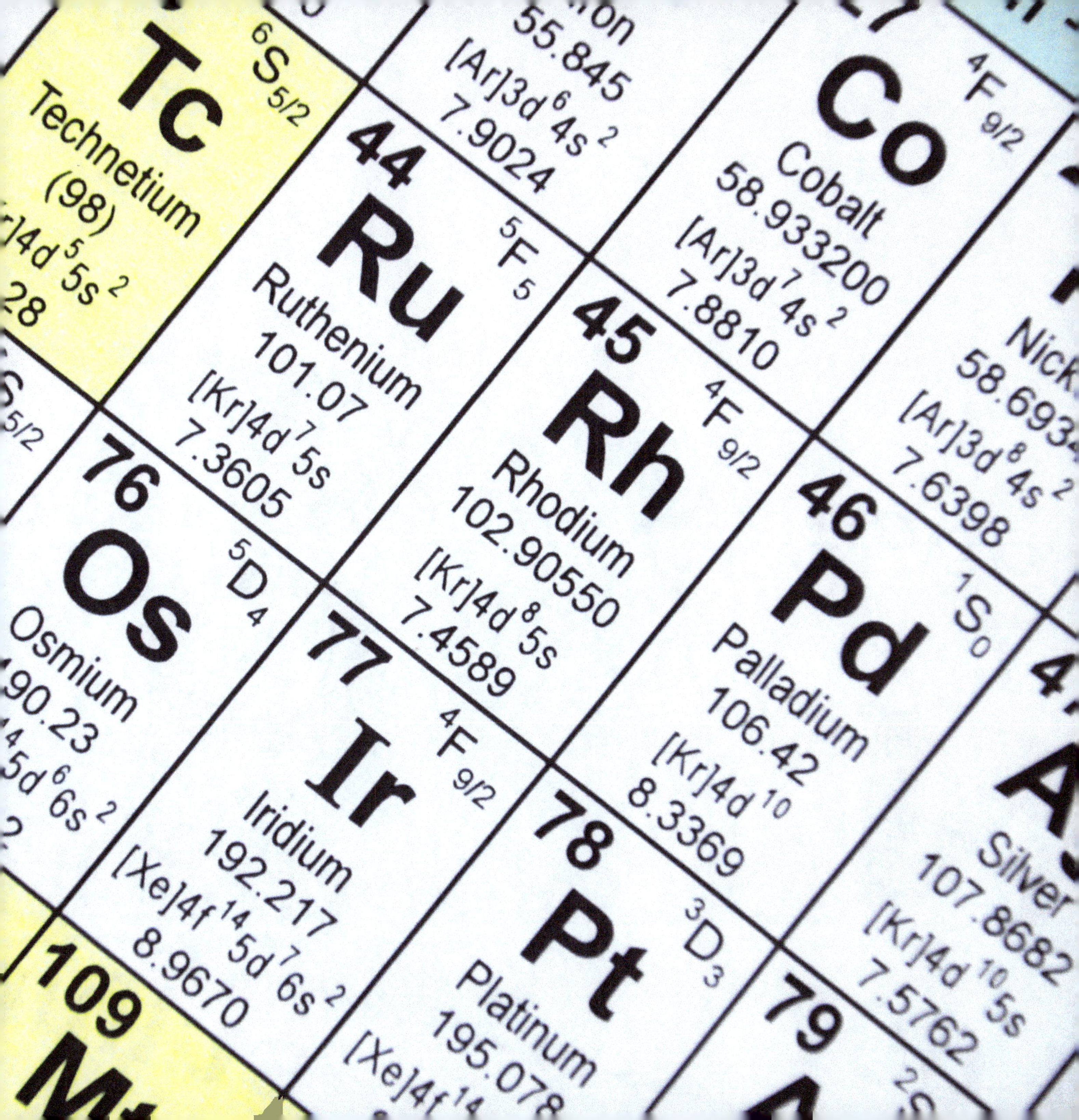

Tc — Technetium (98) [Kr]4d^5 5s^2

^{6}S$_{5/2}$

44 Ru Ruthenium 101.07 [Kr]4d^7 5s 7.3605 — ^{5}F$_5$ 7.9024

Co Cobalt 58.933200 [Ar]3d^7 4s^2 7.8810 — ^{4}F$_{9/2}$ [Ar]3d^6 4s^2 55.845

45 Rh Rhodium 102.90550 [Kr]4d^8 5s 7.4589 — ^{4}F$_{9/2}$

46 Pd Palladium 106.42 [Kr]4d^{10} 8.3369 — ^{1}S$_0$

Nickel 58.693... [Ar]3d^8 4s^2 7.6398

76 Os Osmium 190.23 [Xe]4f^{14} 5d^6 6s^2 — ^{5}D$_4$

77 Ir Iridium 192.217 [Xe]4f^{14} 5d^7 6s^2 8.9670 — ^{4}F$_{9/2}$

78 Pt Platinum 195.078 [Xe]4f^{14} — ^{3}D$_3$

Silver 107.8682 [Kr]4d^{10} 5s 7.5762 — ^{2}S

109 Mt

79 A...

rogen
7
N
1.007
oxygen
8
O
15.999
sulfur

WHAT IS AN ELEMENT?

A single type of atom can make up an element. An element is a pure substance. Elements that are joined together become building blocks of matter in the universe.

Examples of elements are Oxygen, Gold, Helium, and Iron. Each element has an important number which is called atomic number. An atomic number is unique in an element.

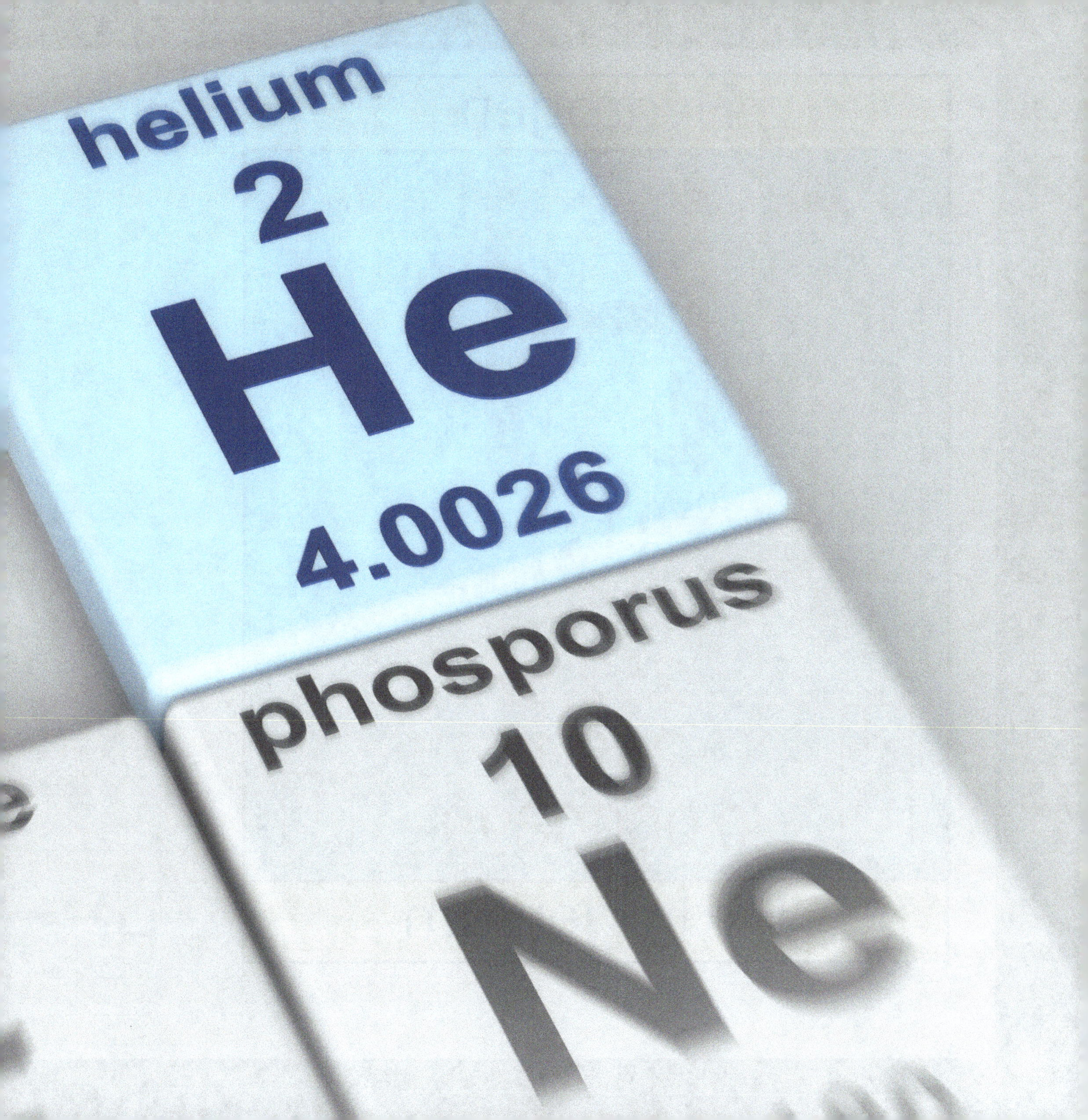

helium
2
He
4.0026
phosporus
10
Ne

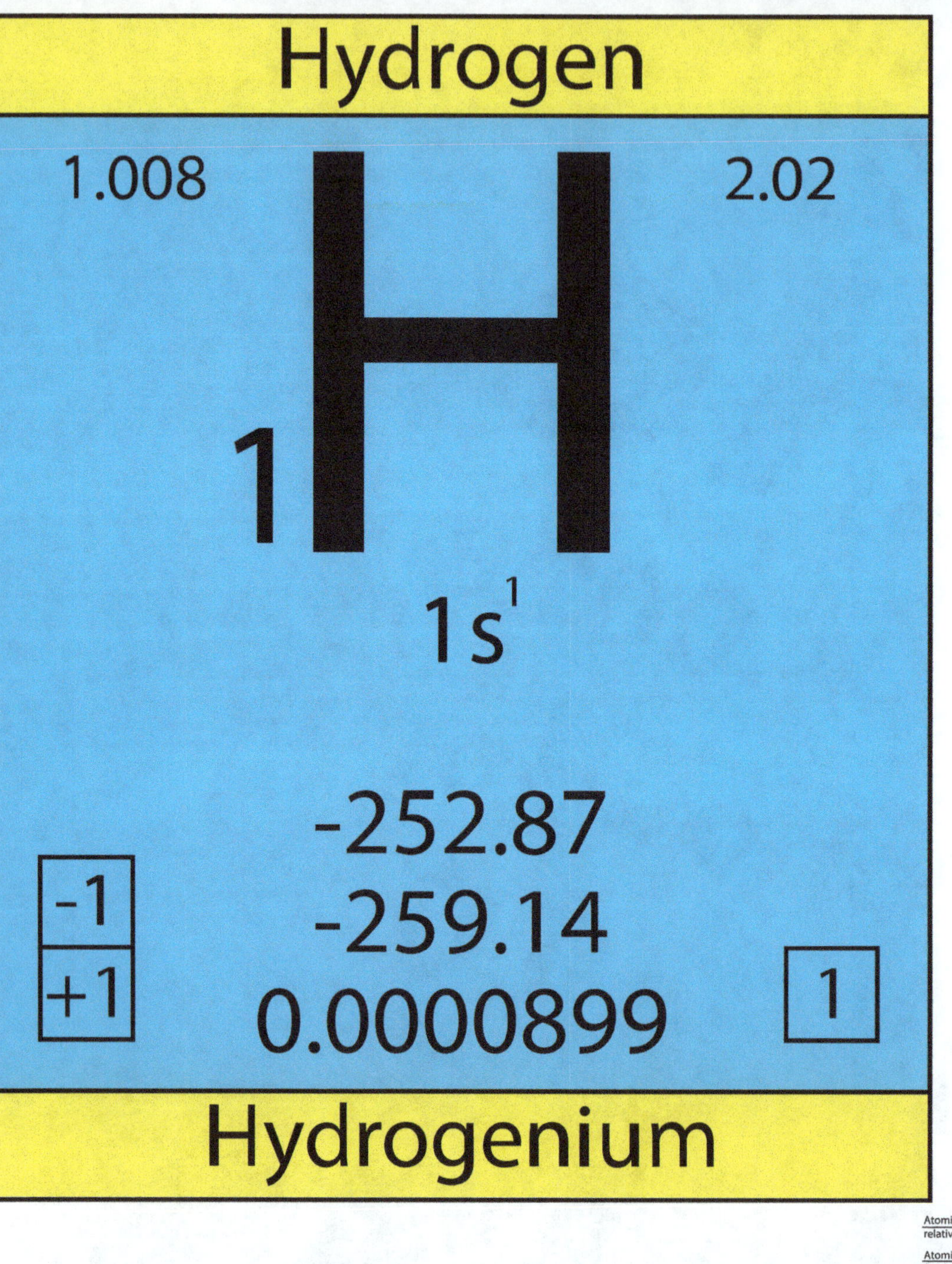
Hydrogen
1.008
2.02
H
1
1s1
-252.87
-259.14
0.0000899
-1
+1
1
Hydrogenium
Hydrogen
1.00794
2.02
H
1
1s1
-252.87
-259.14
0.0000899
-1
+1
1
Hydrogenium
Name
Electronegativity Pauling
Electron confguration
Melting point (C)
Boiling point (C)
Density, g/cm
Distribution of electrons
Latin name
Atomic mass relative
Atomic No Symbol
Oxidation states

This means that no two elements have the same atomic number. The first element is hydrogen. It consists of only one proton. Therefore, its atomic number is 1.

Let's talk about the spectacular families of elements. Are you ready?

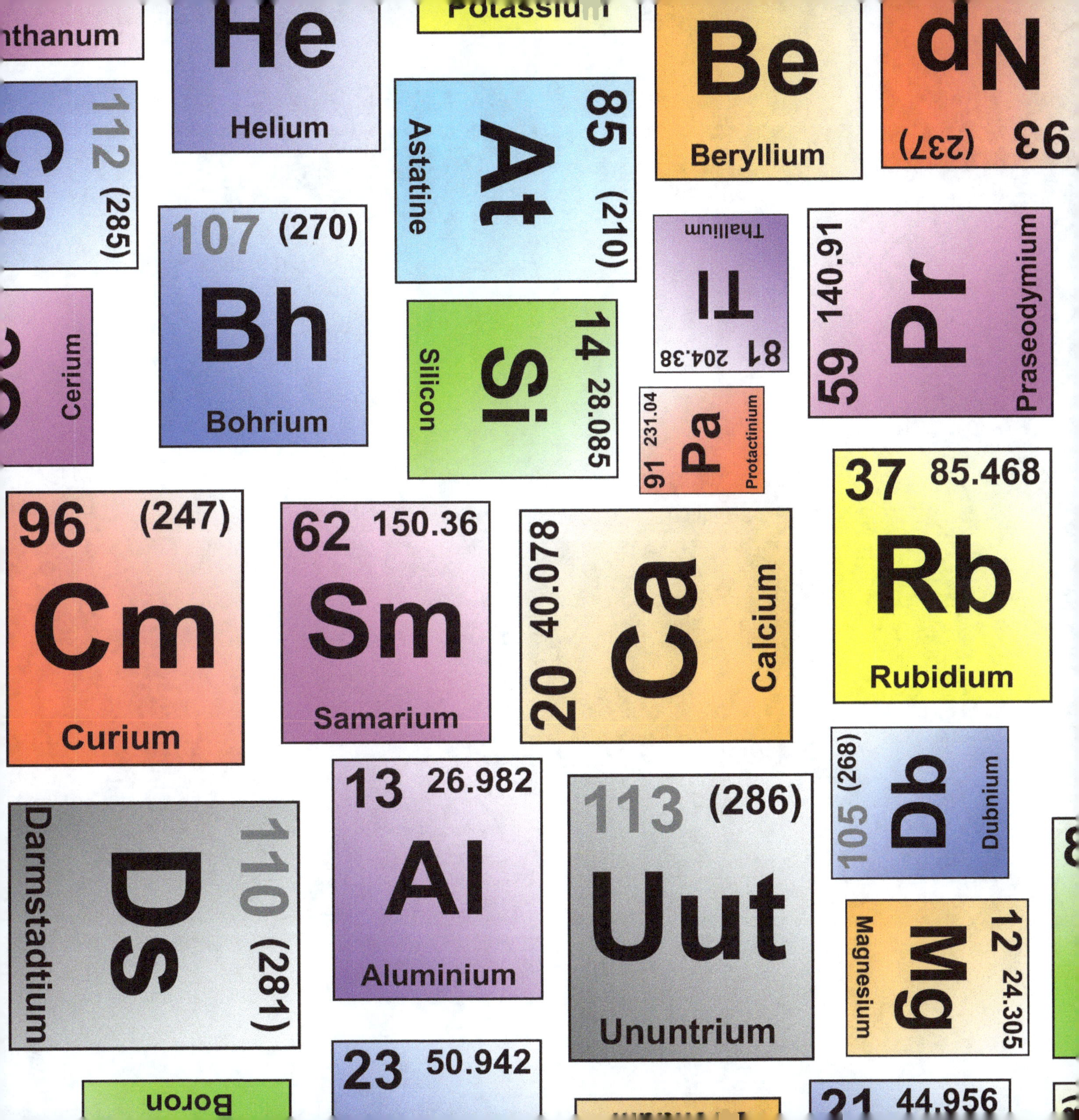
nthanum
112 (285)
Cn
Cerium
He
Helium
85 (210)
At
Astatine
Potassium
Be
Beryllium
Np
93 (237)
107 (270)
Bh
Bohrium
14 28.085
Si
Silicon
Tl
81 204.38
Thallium
59 140.91
Pr
Praseodymium
91 231.04
Pa
Protactinium
37 85.468
Rb
Rubidium
96 (247)
Cm
Curium
62 150.36
Sm
Samarium
20 40.078
Ca
Calcium
13 26.982
Al
Aluminium
113 (286)
Uut
Ununtrium
105 (268)
Db
Dubnium
110 (281)
Ds
Darmstadtium
12 24.305
Mg
Magnesium
23 50.942
Boron
21 44.956

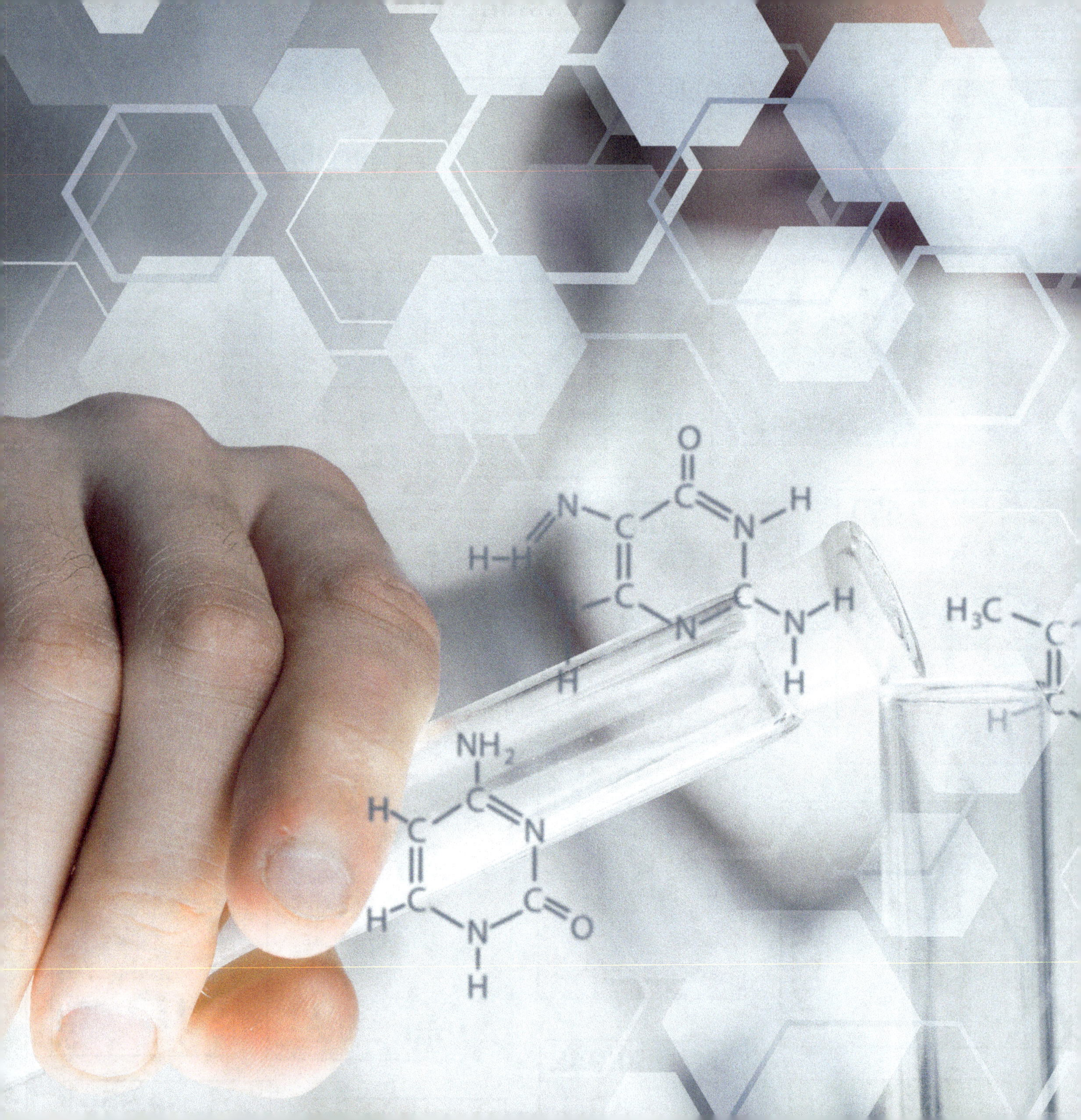

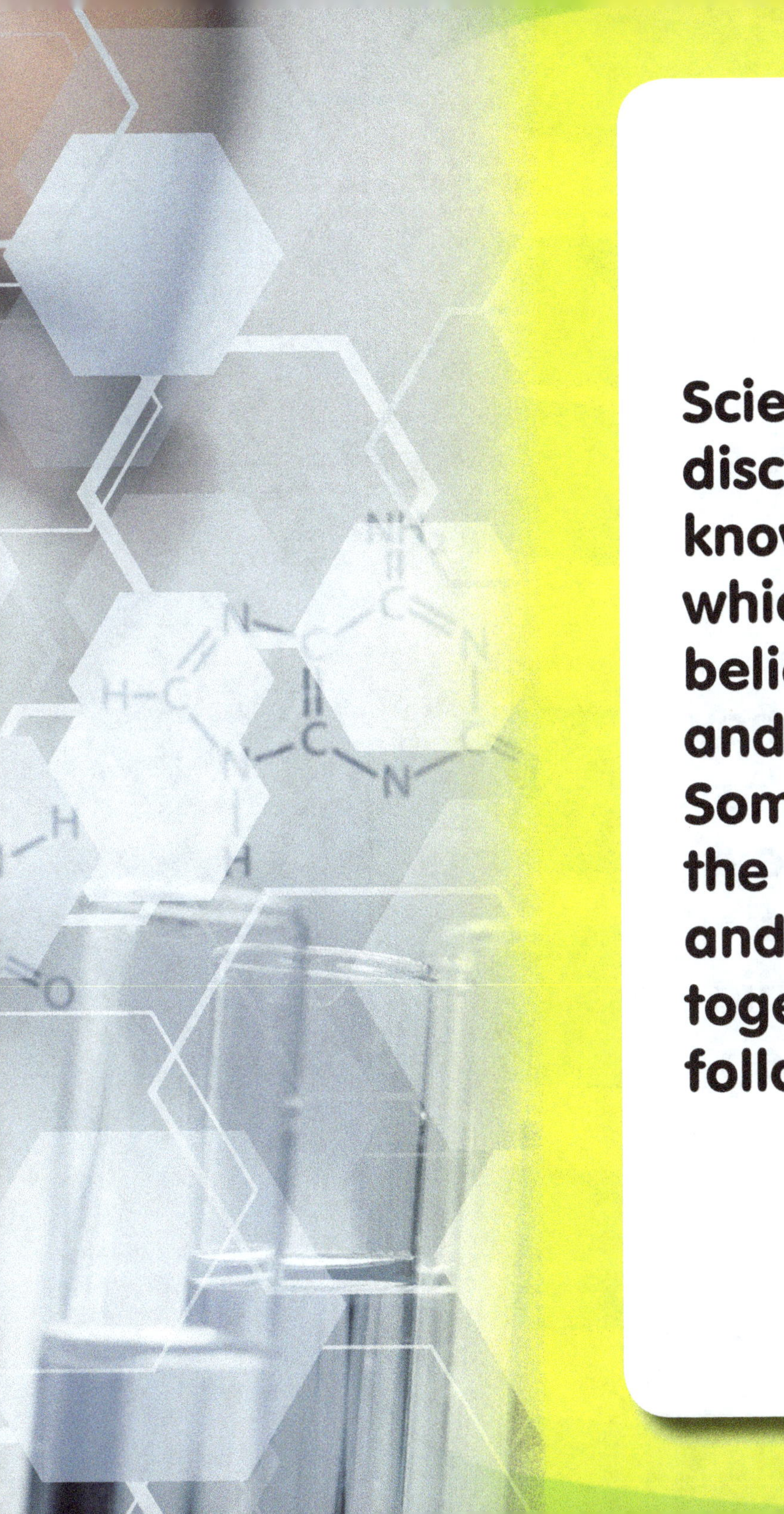

Scientists have discovered a total 118 known elements, of which, 94 elements were believed to be natural and belong to Earth. Some elements have the same properties and they are grouped together, like the following:

ALKALI METALS

These are highly reactive elements in the periodic table. They are also considered as explosive metals. They are found in the first column of the periodic table except hydrogen.

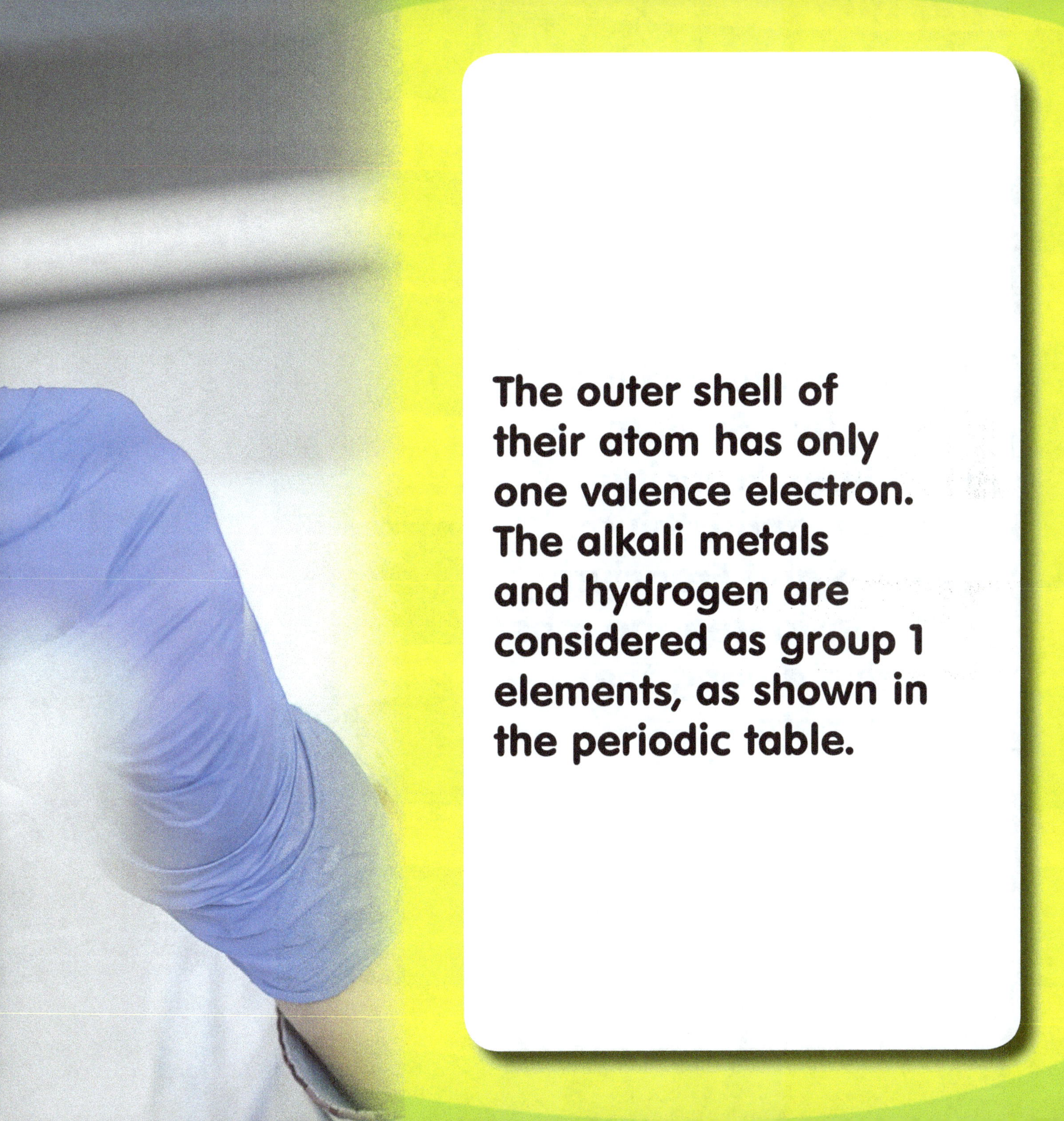
The outer shell of
their atom has only
one valence electron.
The alkali metals
and hydrogen are
considered as group 1
elements, as shown in
the periodic table.

Alkali metals include Potassium, Sodium, Rubidium, Francium, Cesium, and Lithium. Cesium and Francium are considered the most reactive among the alkali metals.

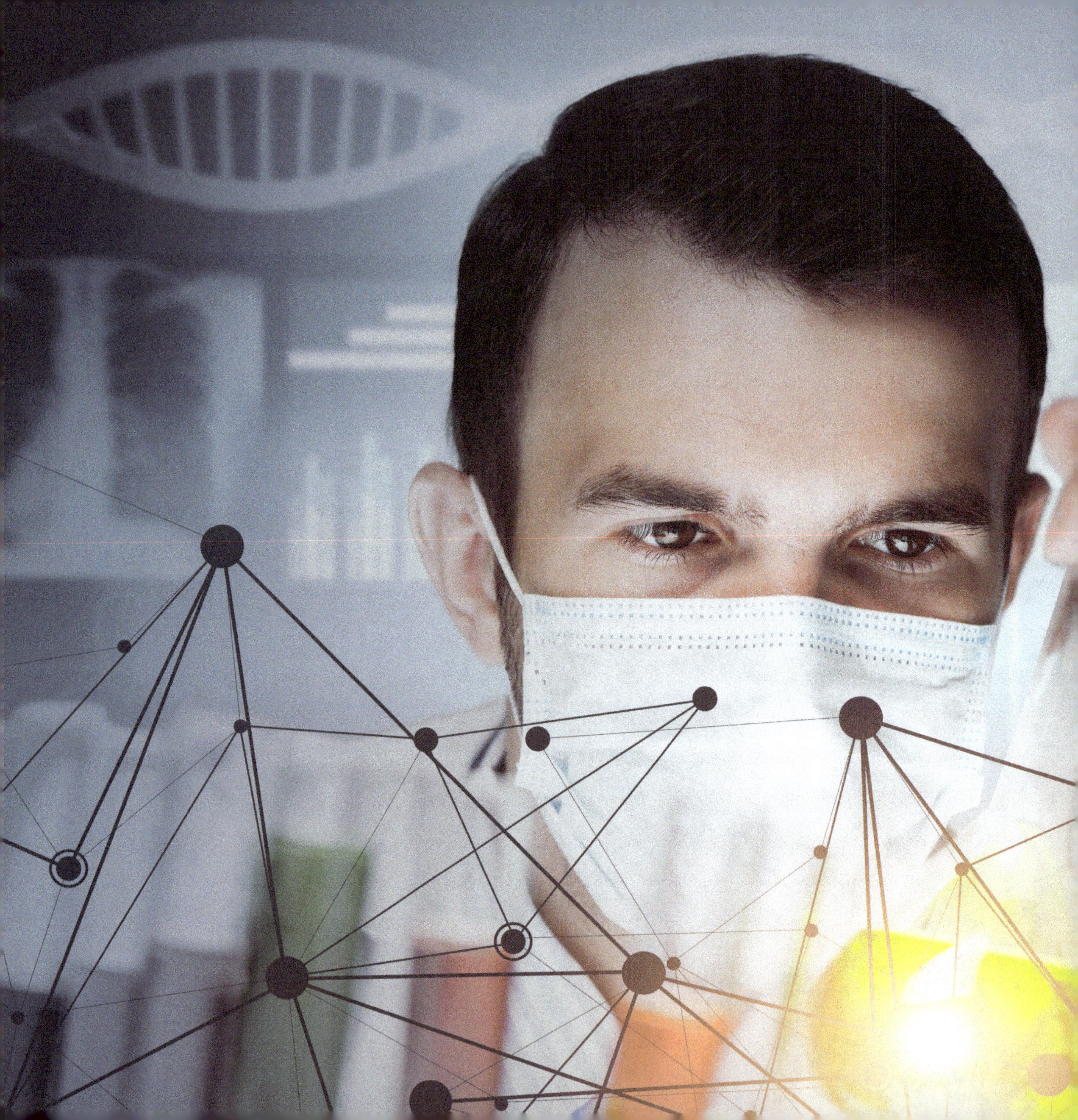

Alkali metals are described to have similar properties. These elements are soft and shiny metals. These soft elements tarnish and react with water when exposed to air.

It is because of oxidation. Alkali metals are good conductors of electricity and heat. They are usually available as salts, not as free elements. Alkali metals are highly reactive with water and air, thus, they are generally stored in oil.

Sodium and Potassium are elements that are considered very important in biological life on the planet. They are very important to life on Earth. The word "alkali" is taken from an Arabic word which means ashes.

When alkali metals are burnt, each of them produce an amazing flame color. Potassium produces lilac-colored flame while Sodium produces orange-colored flame.

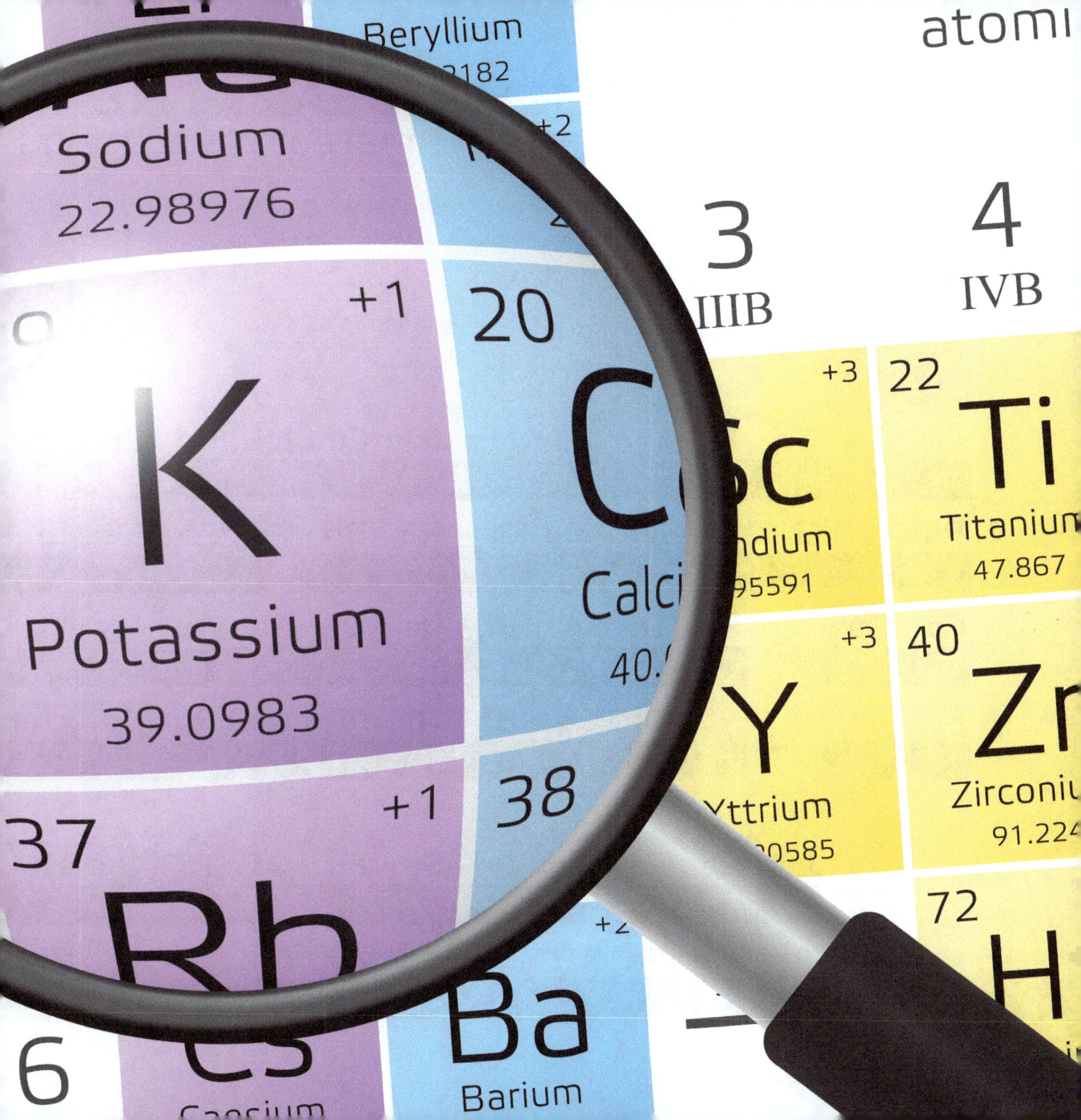
Beryllium
atomi
Sodium
22.98976
+2
3
IIIB
4
IVB
+1
20
K
C
+3
Sc
22
Ti
Potassium
Calci
ndium
Titanium
39.0983
40.
95591
47.867
+3
40
Y
Zr
+1
38
37
Yttrium
Zirconiu
Rb
05585
91.224
72
6
Ba
H
Barium

ALKALINE EARTH METAL

PERIODIC TABLE OF THE ELEMENTS

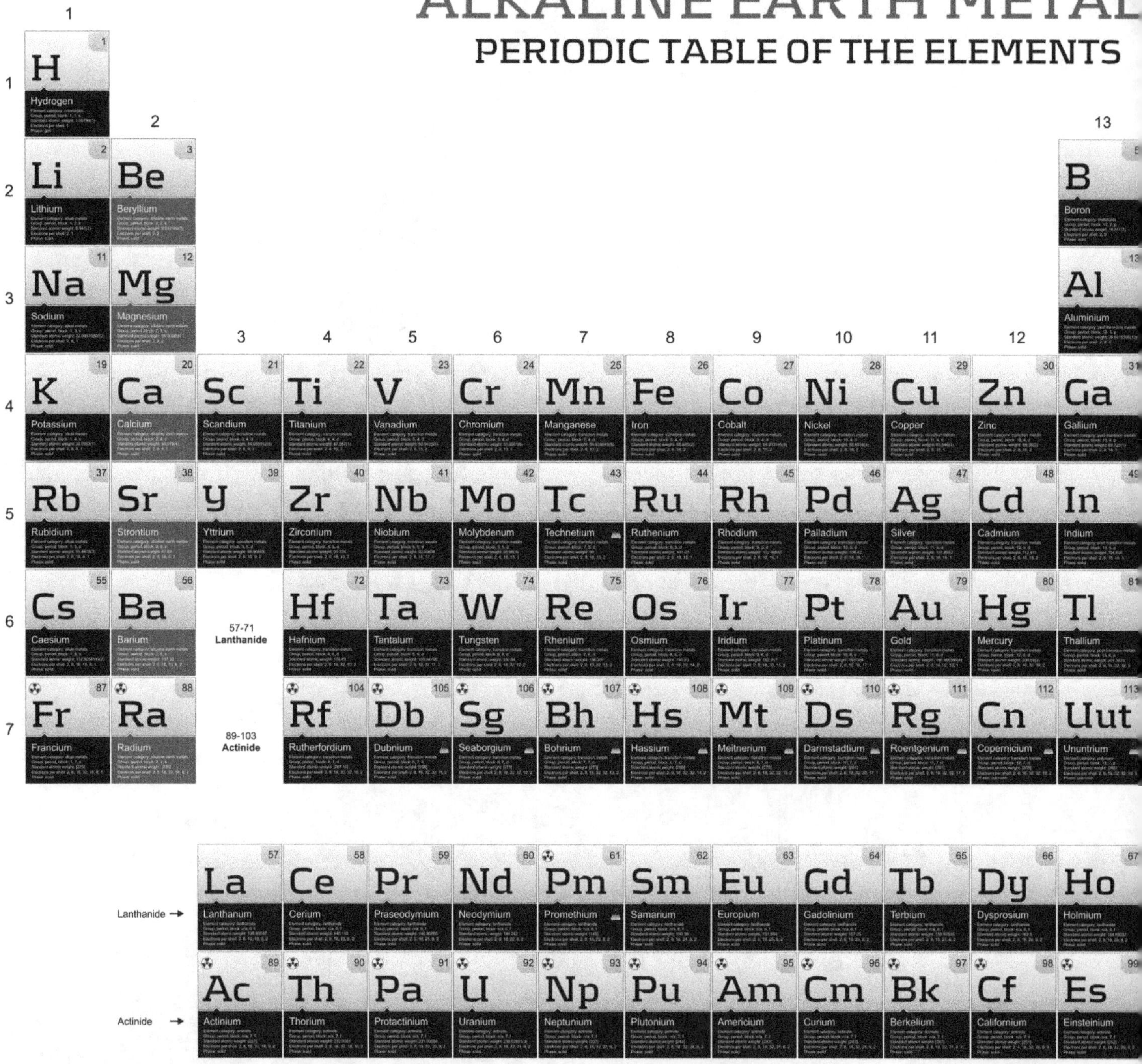

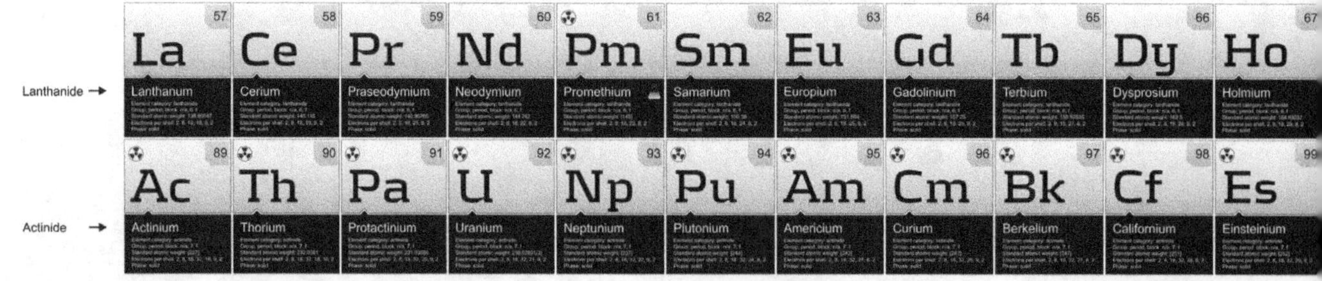

ALKALINE EARTH METALS

These belong to group 2 elements in the Periodic Table and are located in the second column. The Alkaline Earth metals are Magnesium, Beryllium, Calcium, Magnesium, Barium, Strontium, and Radium.

These elements are shiny, silvery and soft metals. They are characterized to have two outer valence electrons which are found in compounds and minerals.

manganese
25
Mn
54.938
iron
26
Fe
55.845
cobalt
27
Co
58.933
nickel
28
Ni
58.693
copper
29
Cu
63.546
zinc
30
Zn
65.38
gallium
3
G
technetium
43
Tc
[98]
ruthenium
44
Ru
101.07
rhodium
45
Rh
102.91
palladium
46
Pd
106.42
silver
47
Ag
107.87
cadmium
48
Cd
112.41
rhenium
75
Re
186.21
osmium
76
Os
190.23
iridium
77
Ir
192.22
platinum
78
Pt
195.08
gold
79
Au
196.97
mercury
80
Hg
200.59
bohrium
107
Bh
[264]
hassium
108
Hs
[277]
meitnerium
[268]
darmstadtium
110
Ds
[271]
roentgenium
111
Rg
[272]
samarium
63
europium
63
gadolinium
64
terbium
65
T

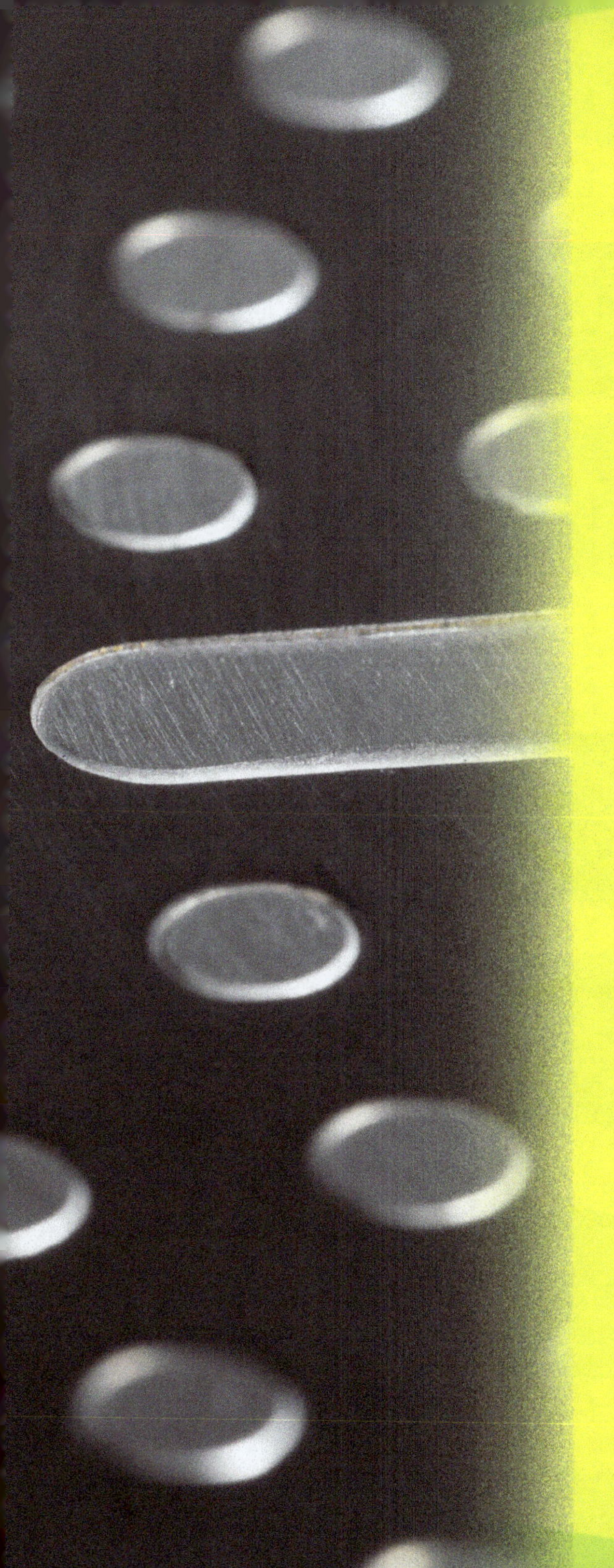

These metals take place in nature and are reactive on certain conditions. They react with water except Beryllium. Calcium is the most abundant Alkaline Earth Metal.

Calcium and
Magnesium are
two very important
elements for animal
and plant life. Calcium,
for example, is highly
needed to build strong
bones and regulate our
body's temperature.

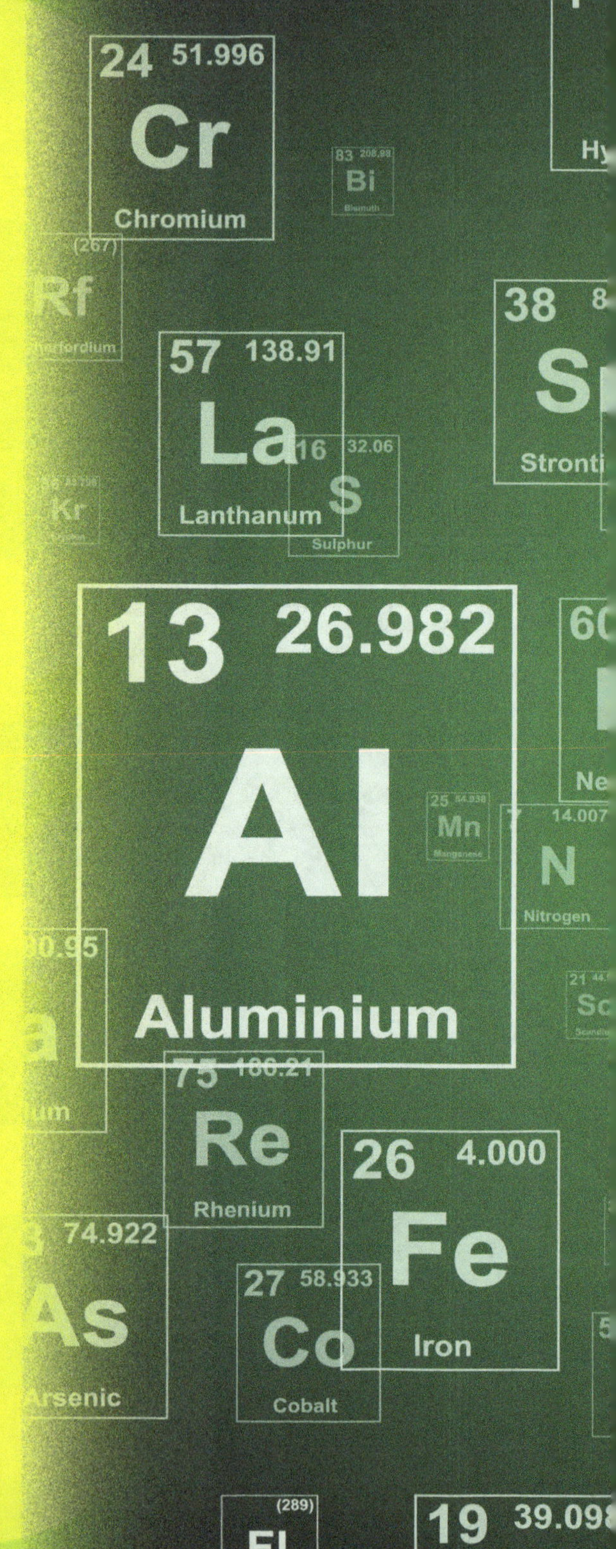

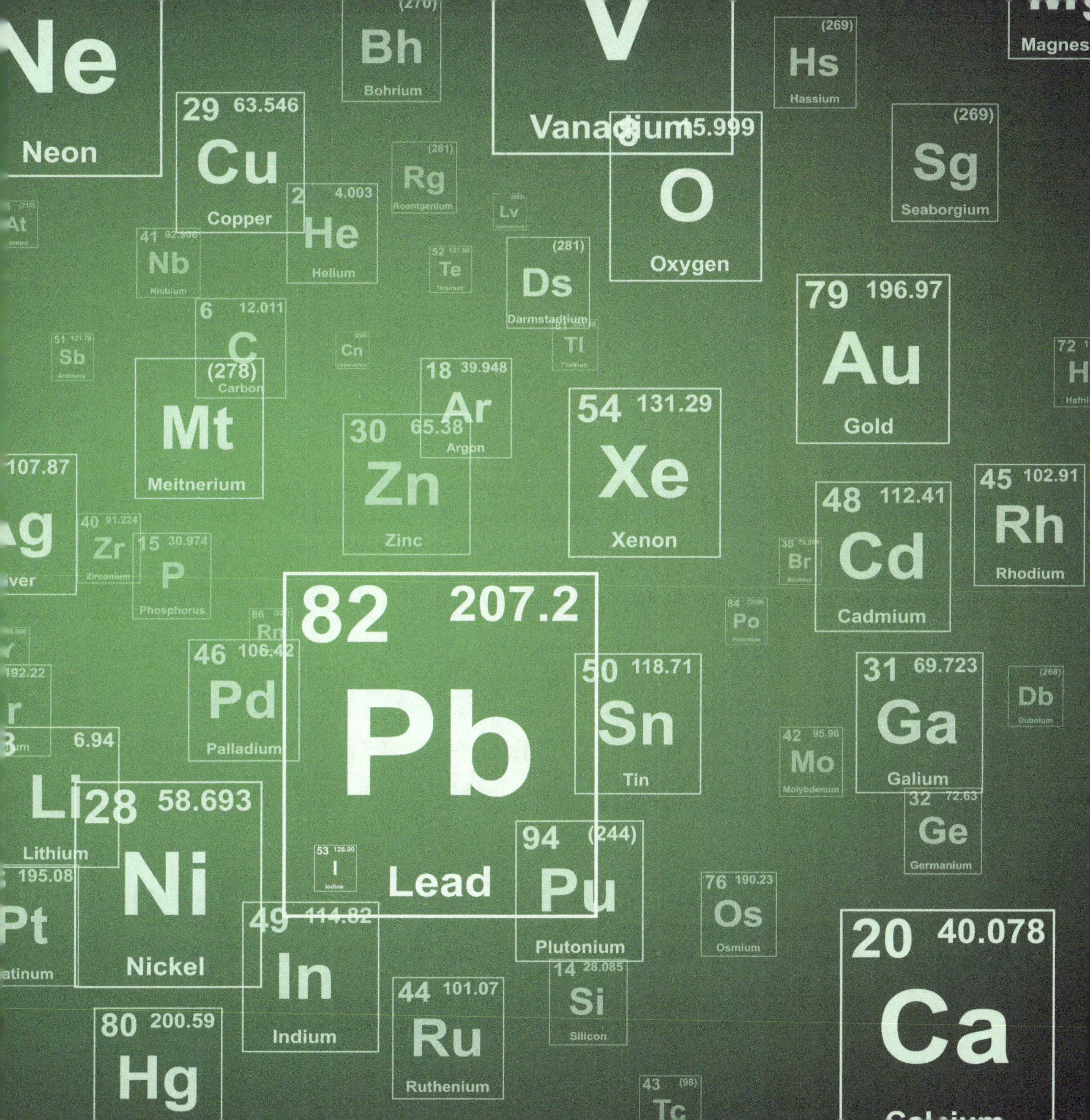

TRANSITION METALS
PERIODIC TABLE OF THE ELEMENTS

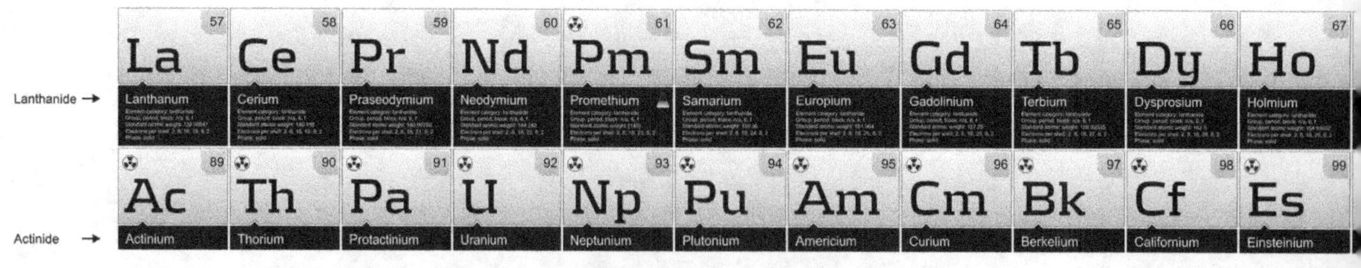

TRANSITION METALS

The following are examples of transition metals in the periodic table of elements: Titanium, Copper, Nickel, Silver, Platinum, and Gold. They are referred to as the "d-block" which has 35 total elements.

They are considered as Group 3 elements in the Periodic Table. These elements are found at the center of the Periodic Table occupying the principal section including columns 3 through 12.

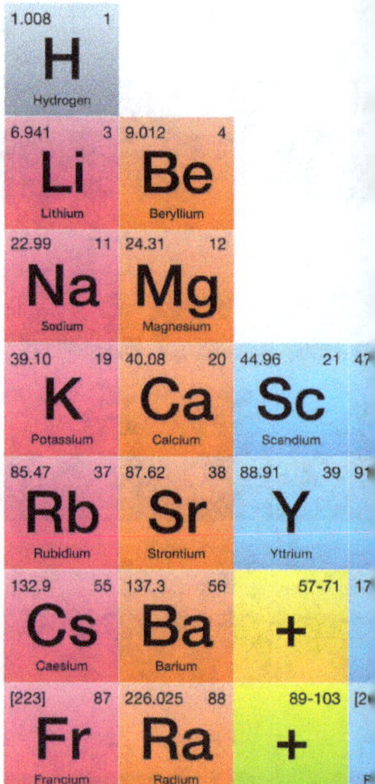

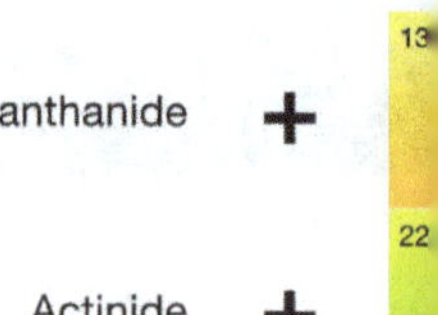

C TABLE OF THE ELEMENTS

Atomic number
·1.008   1
H
Symbol
Name
Hydrogen

4,0026	2
He	
Helium	

10,811	5	12,011	6	14,007	7	15,999	8	18,998	9	20,179	10
B		C		N		O		F		Ne	
Boron		Carbon		Nitrogen		Oxygen		Fluorine		Neon	

26.98	13	28,086	14	30.97	15	32,066	16	35,452	17	39,948	18
Al		Si		P		S		Cl		Ar	
Aluminium		Silicon		Phosphorus		Sulfur		Chlorine		Argon	

23 52.00	24 54.94	25 55.85	26 58.93	27 58.69	28 63.55	29 65.38	30 69.72	31 72.63	32 74.92	33 78.96	34 79,904	35 83,80	36
Cr	Mn	Fe	Co	Ni	Cu	Zn	Ga	Ge	As	Se	Br	Kr	
Chromium	Manganese	Iron	Cobalt	Nickel	Copper	Zinc	Gallium	Germanium	Arsenic	Selenium	Bromine	Krypton	

41 92.91	42 97,907	43 101.1	44 102.9	45 106.4	46 107.9	47 112.4	48 114.8	49 118.7	50 121.8	51 127.6	52 126,905	53 131,29	54
Mo	Tc	Ru	Rh	Pd	Ag	Cd	In	Sn	Sb	Te	I	Xe	
Molybdenum	Technetium	Ruthenium	Rhodium	Palladium	Silver	Cadmium	Indium	Tin	Antimony	Tellurium	Iodine	Xenon	

73 180.9	74 186.2	75 190.2	76 192.2	77 195.1	78 197.0	79 200.6	80 204,383	81 207.2	82 209.0	83 [209]	84 [210]	85 [222]	86
W	Re	Os	Ir	Pt	Au	Hg	Tl	Pb	Bi	Po	At	Rn	
Tungsten	Rhenium	Osmium	Iridium	Platinum	Gold	Mercury	Thallium	Lead	Bismuth	Polonium	Astatine	Radon	

105 [271]	106 [267]	107 [269]	108 [276]	109 [281]	110 [281]	111 [285]	112 [284]	113 [289]	114 [288]	115 [293]	116 [294]	117 [294]	118
Sg	Bh	Hs	Mt	Ds	Rg	Cn	Uut	Fl	Uup	Lv	Uus	Uuo	
Seaborgium	Bohrium	Hassium	Meitnerium	Darmstadtium	Roentgenium	Copernicium	Ununtrium	Flerovium	Ununpentium	Livermorium	Ununseptium	Ununoctium	

58 140,908	59 144,24	60 144,913	61 150,36	62 151,965	63 157,25	64 158,925	65 162,50	66 164,93	67 167,26	68 168,934	69 173,04	70 174,967	71
Pr	Nd	Pm	Sm	Eu	Gd	Tb	Dy	Ho	Er	Tm	Yb	Lu	
Praseodymium	Neodymium	Promethium	Samarium	Europium	Gadolinium	Terbium	Dysprosium	Holmium	Erbium	Thulium	Ytterbium	Lutetium	

90 231,036	91 238,029	92 237,048	93 244,064	94 243,061	95 247,07	96 247,07	97 251,08	98 252,083	99 257,095	100 258,1	101 259,1	102 262,11	103
Pa	U	Np	Pu	Am	Cm	Bk	Cf	Es	Fm	Md	No	Lr	
Protactinium	Uranium	Neptunium	Plutonium	Americium	Curium	Berkelium	Californium	Einsteinium	Fermium	Mendelevium	Nobelium	Lawrencium	

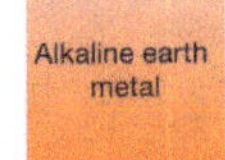
Alkaline earth metal

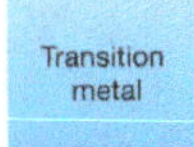
Transition metal

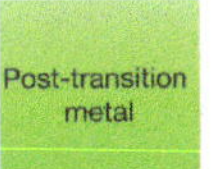
Post-transition metal

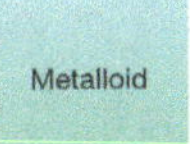
Metalloid

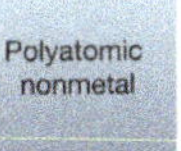
Polyatomic nonmetal

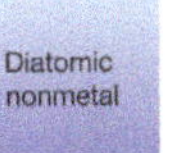
Diatomic nonmetal

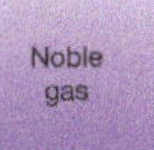
Noble gas

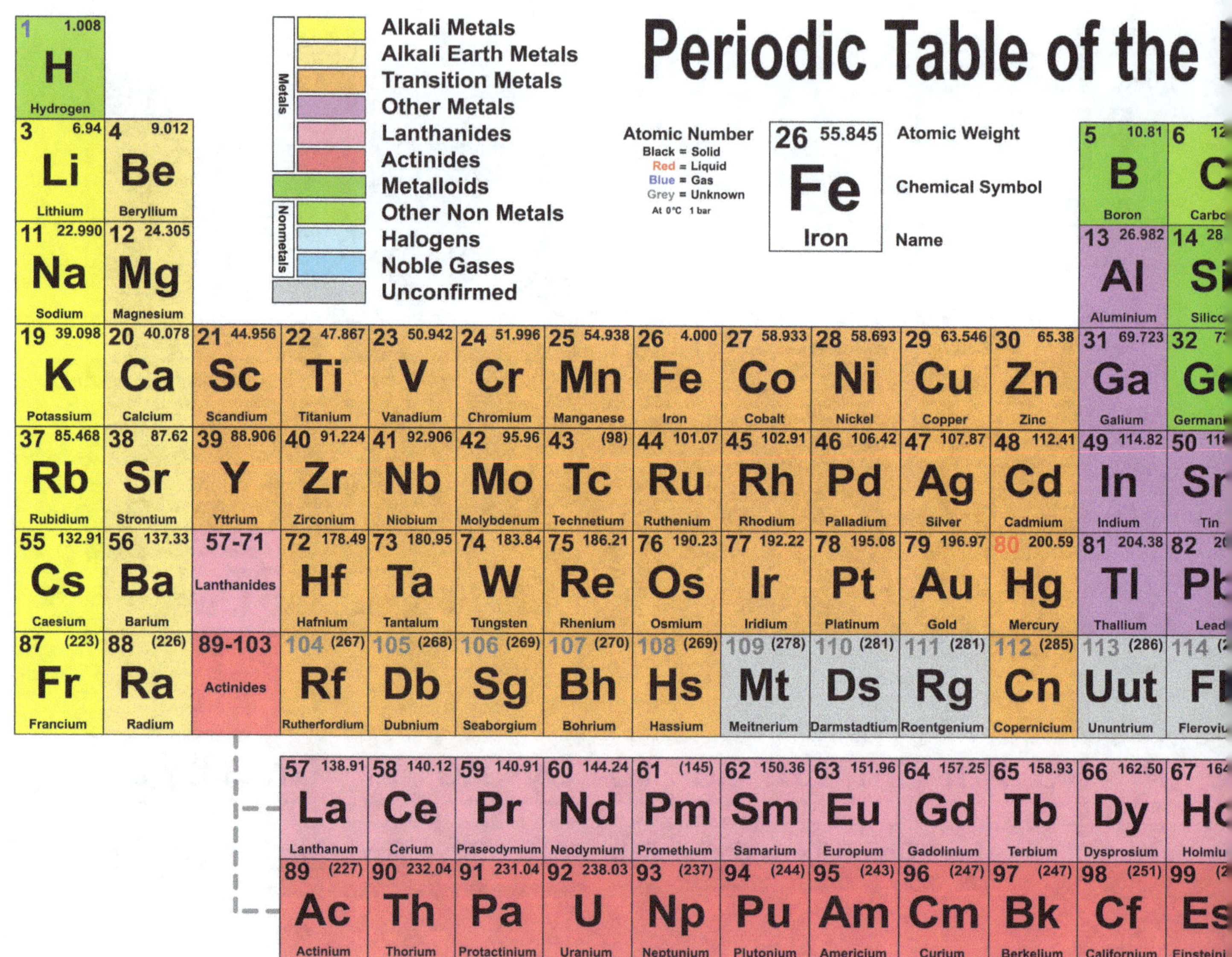
Periodic Table of the
Alkali Metals
Alkali Earth Metals
Transition Metals
Other Metals
Lanthanides
Actinides
Metalloids
Other Non Metals
Halogens
Noble Gases
Unconfirmed
Metals
Nonmetals
Atomic Number
Black = Solid
Red = Liquid
Blue = Gas
Grey = Unknown
At 0°C   1 bar
26   55.845   Atomic Weight
Fe   Chemical Symbol
Iron   Name
1   1.008
H
Hydrogen
3   6.94
Li
Lithium
4   9.012
Be
Beryllium
11   22.990
Na
Sodium
12   24.305
Mg
Magnesium
5   10.81
B
Boron
6   12
C
Carbo
13   26.982
Al
Aluminium
14   28
Si
Silico
19   39.098
K
Potassium
20   40.078
Ca
Calcium
21   44.956
Sc
Scandium
22   47.867
Ti
Titanium
23   50.942
V
Vanadium
24   51.996
Cr
Chromium
25   54.938
Mn
Manganese
26   4.000
Fe
Iron
27   58.933
Co
Cobalt
28   58.693
Ni
Nickel
29   63.546
Cu
Copper
30   65.38
Zn
Zinc
31   69.723
Ga
Galium
32   73
Ge
Germani
37   85.468
Rb
Rubidium
38   87.62
Sr
Strontium
39   88.906
Y
Yttrium
40   91.224
Zr
Zirconium
41   92.906
Nb
Niobium
42   95.96
Mo
Molybdenum
43   (98)
Tc
Technetium
44   101.07
Ru
Ruthenium
45   102.91
Rh
Rhodium
46   106.42
Pd
Palladium
47   107.87
Ag
Silver
48   112.41
Cd
Cadmium
49   114.82
In
Indium
50   118
Sn
Tin
55   132.91
Cs
Caesium
56   137.33
Ba
Barium
57-71
Lanthanides
72   178.49
Hf
Hafnium
73   180.95
Ta
Tantalum
74   183.84
W
Tungsten
75   186.21
Re
Rhenium
76   190.23
Os
Osmium
77   192.22
Ir
Iridium
78   195.08
Pt
Platinum
79   196.97
Au
Gold
80   200.59
Hg
Mercury
81   204.38
Tl
Thallium
82   20
Pb
Lead
87   (223)
Fr
Francium
88   (226)
Ra
Radium
89-103
Actinides
104   (267)
Rf
Rutherfordium
105   (268)
Db
Dubnium
106   (269)
Sg
Seaborgium
107   (270)
Bh
Bohrium
108   (269)
Hs
Hassium
109   (278)
Mt
Meitnerium
110   (281)
Ds
Darmstadtium
111   (281)
Rg
Roentgenium
112   (285)
Cn
Copernicium
113   (286)
Uut
Ununtrium
114
Fl
Flerovium
57   138.91
La
Lanthanum
58   140.12
Ce
Cerium
59   140.91
Pr
Praseodymium
60   144.24
Nd
Neodymium
61   (145)
Pm
Promethium
62   150.36
Sm
Samarium
63   151.96
Eu
Europium
64   157.25
Gd
Gadolinium
65   158.93
Tb
Terbium
66   162.50
Dy
Dysprosium
67   164
Ho
Holmiu
89   (227)
Ac
Actinium
90   232.04
Th
Thorium
91   231.04
Pa
Protactinium
92   238.03
U
Uranium
93   (237)
Np
Neptunium
94   (244)
Pu
Plutonium
95   (243)
Am
Americium
96   (247)
Cm
Curium
97   (247)
Bk
Berkelium
98   (251)
Cf
Californium
99
Es
Einstein

This is how these elements occupy space in the periodic table although the elements in column twelve are occasionally taken as not part of the transition metals like Mercury and Zinc.

Chemists use the "d electron count instead of using valence electrons to describe transition elements. The transition metals are frequently used in different industries because of their unique qualities.

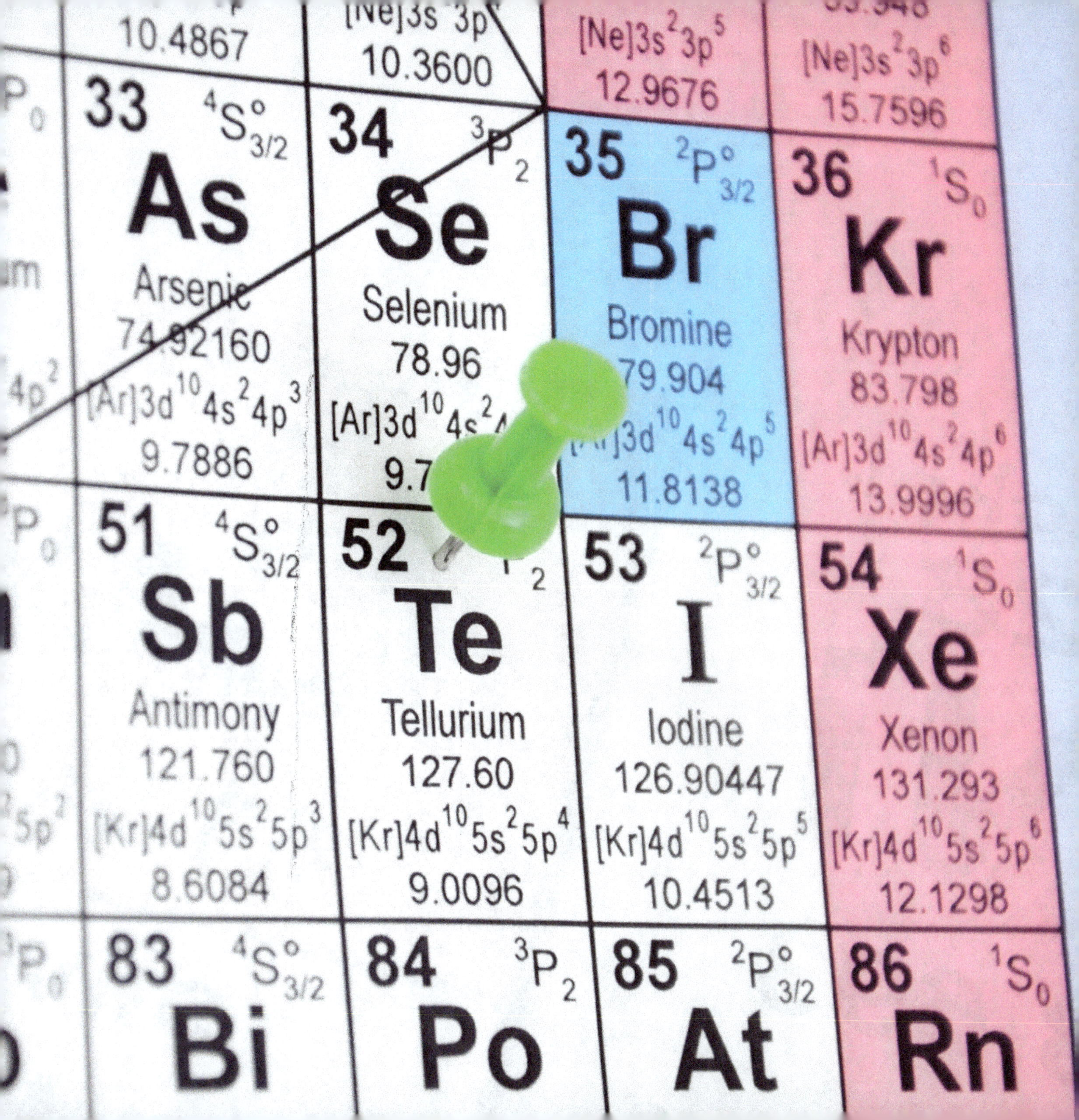

33	34	35	36
10.4867	10.3600	[Ne]3s^{2}3p^5 12.9676	[Ne]3s^{2}3p^6 15.7596
33 $^4S^o_{3/2}$ **As** Arsenic 74.92160 [Ar]3d^{10}4s^{2}4p^3 9.7886	**34** $^3P_2$ **Se** Selenium 78.96 [Ar]3d^{10}4s^{2}4p^4 9.7	**35** $^2P^o_{3/2}$ **Br** Bromine 79.904 [Ar]3d^{10}4s^{2}4p^5 11.8138	**36** $^1S_0$ **Kr** Krypton 83.798 [Ar]3d^{10}4s^{2}4p^6 13.9996
51 $^4S^o_{3/2}$ **Sb** Antimony 121.760 [Kr]4d^{10}5s^{2}5p^3 8.6084	**52** $^3P_2$ **Te** Tellurium 127.60 [Kr]4d^{10}5s^{2}5p^4 9.0096	**53** $^2P^o_{3/2}$ **I** Iodine 126.90447 [Kr]4d^{10}5s^{2}5p^5 10.4513	**54** $^1S_0$ **Xe** Xenon 131.293 [Kr]4d^{10}5s^{2}5p^6 12.1298
83 $^4S^o_{3/2}$ **Bi**	**84** $^3P_2$ **Po**	**85** $^2P^o_{3/2}$ **At**	**86** $^1S_0$ **Rn**

ckel
28
Ni
3.693
copper
29
Cu
63.546
silve

The elements Lanthanides and Actinides are sometimes referred to as transition metals. They are also called inner transition metals. Aside from its outer shell, these elements have incomplete inner subshell.

Transition metals share the same properties like their ability to form compounds with varied colors. They are also conductors of electricity and are paramagnetic. They have high melting and boiling points.

CH₃C—NH₂
C+O₂=CO₂
Ca
Al+2KOH→K₂A
te
Li
2Al(OH)₃→Al₂O₃+3H₂O
Chemist
C=O—NH₂
H₂SO₄
H₃PO₄

The mystery around us has been unfolded before our very eyes through the study of Chemistry. Isn't it wonderful to know how the world works and what it is made of? Chemistry is indeed the study of life and truly interesting to discover.

Visit

BABY PROFESSOR
EDUCATION KIDS

www.BabyProfessorBooks.com

to download Free Baby Professor eBooks
and view our catalog of new and exciting
Children's Books